What I will be teaching in this book will be very simple to understand by all. But if you will just take your time to live them out you'll be amazed at the changes you will experience in your life.

The evidences abound that if you will take the teachings from this book to heart and do what you learn, in a short while you will also be among the many people that have submitted reports of how this book have changed their lives.

Get ready for an experience like you've never had before.

Thank you.
Charles Silva

Introduction of Chapters

This is to intimate us with the courses we will be looking at in this book. Four chapters in all as listed below:

Personal Transformation and Leadership – Parts 1&2
Personal Leadership and Goal Setting – Parts 1&2
Entrepreneurial Mindset – Parts 1&2
Redefining Purpose – Parts 1&2

1. Personal Transformation & Leadership.
More and more people, today, are overwhelmed by the issues of life. Low self-esteem, depression, anxiety, and all the likes are the results of these issues. A lot of people feel they are in one big wheel spun by an invisible hand. Some say we are just pencils in the hands of the creator and we have absolutely no control in how things turn out. But is that true?

In this course we will be going back to the basics of personal transformation and get to see that while there are lots of things over which we may not have any control, we do have control over some other things. And maybe if we begin to focus on the things over which we have control, we will begin to feel less stressed and lead better lives. So we will be looking at the keys to personal transformation.

Man by nature, wants to dominate. We want to have control over our world. There is this feeling of inadequacy when we are not in control.

However, control should begin with oneself. For how can you lead others if you cannot lead yourself? How can you gain control over others if you cannot control yourself?

Personal Leadership is a book which is set out to teach you the principles of personal leadership. So we can begin from the beginning.

We live in an age where everything seems to have advanced, everything except one. Trips that used to take months two hundred years ago are now travelled in hours. Tasks that used to take almost eternity are now accomplished almost immediately. Man, through the aid of technology, has redefined life. Things our ancestors tagged impossible we now take for granted. Indeed life has advanced beyond imagination. But even though technology has made us accomplish great feats, has man, himself, really improved much?

The most popular quote on leadership today is, "Everything rises and falls on leadership." What many of us have not realized is that the quote is not saying everything rises and falls on the leader alone, even though that is also true to a large extent, but everything rises and falls on "leadership". If you don't know how to lead, everything around you will fall. And like John Maxwell said, the first person you should lead is yourself. But can you honestly say you are doing a good job at leading yourself?

In life, anyone can talk but only few really take the necessary steps to achieve what they talk about. The problem with many of us in this part of the world is that we tend to want to do by prayer what an increase in capacity should do for us. I believe in prayer but I also know that we have brains for a reason.

We live in an age where information thrives and almost everyone has become an expert in one area or another. The downside is that most people now think they already know all they need to know. And the day you think you know it all is the day your landing approach begins.

My name is Charles Silva and I am the Author of this book.

In this course we will be using the bible as our reference. Not as a religious book, though, but as a book that really contains principles that are relevant to the subject.

2. Personal Leadership & Goal Setting

Goal setting has been a major issue in the leadership world and different authorities proffer different methods. Over the years, the methods have evolved. What is becoming clear is that there is no one-size-fits-all method. Industrialization may have made it possible for a production line to churn out a particular product for everyone to use. But when it comes to the issues of life it does not work that way.

In this course we will get to understand the relevance of personal leadership in goal setting. It will introduce a concept where you can tailor-make your own program to achieve your goal. We will look at various application of this concept and why the traditional method of goal setting, popularly called the SMART method, has a high failure rate when applied in personal goals.

The major reference material for this course will be Small Move Big Change by Caroline L. Arnold.

3. Entrepreneurial Mindset

The world is run by entrepreneurs. Even though many people dream to work with global giants, the global economy actually runs on small and medium scale companies. SMEs generate more employment overall than the global giants. But whether Multinationals or SMEs, entrepreneurs are at the top of the chain.

What sort of mindset do entrepreneurs have? Are they really special like some journals claim? Are they moulded from a unique stone? Or are they just like the rest of us? These questions and more are what we will be answering in this course.

4. Redefining Purpose

The concept of Purpose is a very intriguing one. At one extreme are people who believe life is a free-for-all affair. At the other end are those who believe that every single thing you do has to be dictated by your purpose - the color of your shoe, the color of the dress you wear in the morning, what you have for breakfast, EVERYTHING. So the phrase "Discovering Purpose" has become one scary term especially among Christians.

There are many people who go through life trying to discover purpose until they hit the grave. But what really is Purpose? Is it something we have to fast and pray to discover or is there something we are missing? Redefining Purpose aims to answer all of these questions and more.

It's an honor to have every one of you in this class. I promise to give my very best and with God's help all your expectations will be met.

Chapter One

Personal Transformation and Leadership - Part 1

The reason why many of us don't see the desired results in our lives is not because what we have learnt over the years does not work. It is actually because of our attitude towards what we have learnt.

When most people listen to speakers or read books, in their minds are things like, "I have heard that before, say something new." Our lives do not change because we hear something new but because we have made use of what we have learnt.

Instead of "I have heard that before," ask yourself, "Have I mastered this?" "Does my life prove that I have mastered this?" "Do my finances prove that I have mastered this?" "Does my waistline prove that I have mastered this?" Asking questions like these give you a paradigm shift in your thinking.

I say this because if you have read some of the reports from people that have been through this class you will be tempted to think I teach one thing that nobody has learnt before. But that is not true. What I teach is out there for everyone to read and learn.

The only difference is that I have this gift of simplifying things. It's just something that comes to me naturally.

Probably because one of my core values is simplicity. But it just so happens that when people read my books they have better understanding.

So as you read through this book, they may be simple but they are powerful. Please don't take them for granted even if you have heard them before. Let your focus be on how you can apply them in your life.

INTRODUCTION: A STETHOSCOPE DOES NOT MAKE a MEDICAL DOCTOR.

What makes a medical doctor? Is it the title Dr. before the name of the person or something more than the title? Someone goes into medical school and stays in there for several years and when they come out they listen to the way someone else is breathing and says to him, "You have an issue with your lungs." The person says, "I'm OK." But the doctor says, "No, you're not okay. Something is wrong with your lungs; you need to have some tests done."

It turns out that the doctor is right. While in Med School, the doctor was TRAINED to see things the average person will not see. To listen to sounds the way the average person doesn't. And after several years of TRAINING the doctor has been CONDITIONED TO FUNCTION BY DEFAULT in the new way he or she has been trained.

So we can say the difference between a doctor and a lawyer is not the stethoscope, it is in who they are. The difference is in their person. Hanging a stethoscope around your neck does not make you a medical doctor.

A POPULAR LEADERSHIP QUOTE

There is a leadership quote that has become a cliché everywhere in the world today. It was made popular by John Maxwell. It is the quote "Everything rises and falls on leadership." The very first application of that quote is in our individual lives. How well do I lead myself? That is the right question to ask because everything in my life will rise or fall based on my leadership ability.

How do you expect a man who at every opportunity he gets wants to satisfy his selfish desires, now lead an organization or a nation well? When we expect those people who are at the top of the leadership cadre in the nation to do excellently well, we are expecting too much from them. Most of them have not been able to lead themselves how then can we expect them to lead the nation well?

WHAT DOES GOD'S WORD SAY ABOUT THE MIND?
Rom 12:2
"Don't copy the behavior and customs of this world, but let God transform you into a new person by CHANGING THE WAY YOU THINK. Then you will know what God wants you to do…" (NLT)

You must make a deliberate effort not to think the way the world thinks. You must disconnect yourself from the what-will-people-say mentality. Popularity comes cheap. All you have to do to be popular is to do things the way they want you to do them. True significance does not come that cheap. But the beautiful part is that when you are significant fame will come along with it. And significance is first achieved on the inside.

In this course, Personal Transformation and Leadership we will be looking at how we can make the paradigm shift we need to be able to lead ourselves and consequently lead others. I want to urge you to take seriously what you are about to learn. It changed my life. The principles I will be sharing in this course are not new. I learnt them and I have taught these same principles in as I go out to speak to people around the world and the reports have been remarkably consistent.

I must also say, however, that though the principles themselves are easy, it will take a high degree of self-discipline to put them into practice in your lives. Practicing them won't be easy because of the so many distractions in the world today. But if you will exercise the self-discipline needed to practice the principles, they will soon become your way of life. Let us now go proper into the subject matter.

IT BEGINS IN YOUR MIND
Prov. 23:7
"For as a man thinks in his heart, so is he." (NKJV)

Life is a lot like sailing. You don't have control over the wind but you have control over the sails. The angle in which you position the sails determines where the wind will take you. If you focus all your energy around the things you have no control over, you are signing a contract with frustration. It is like trying to control of the wind. But if you focus on adjusting the sails, then the wind which you don't have control over will take you to your desired destination.

In this life there is only one thing you have absolute control over and that is yourself. You don't have absolute control over anything else, not even your spouse. But when you exercise the right control over yourself, all other external factors will fall in line to take you to where you want to be.

So, Personal Leadership is about taking control over yourself. Why? Because the same wind blows on everybody and you cannot control the wind. And to take control over yourself begins with taking control over your thoughts. The way you think.

YOUR HEART AFFECTS YOUR LIFE
Prov. 4:23
"Above all else, guard your heart, for it affects EVERYTHING you do." (NLT)

Matt. 12:35
"The good man from his inner good treasure flings forth good

things, and the evil man out of his inner evil storehouse flings forth evil things." (AMP)

WHAT YOU HAVE STORED UP IN YOUR HEART OVER TIME IS WHAT YOU ARE CURRENTLY EXPERIENCING IN YOUR LIFE. When what you've stored up in your heart is good, you will experience good things in your life. Your external will always measure up to your internal make-up. Therefore the man who wants to experience good things in his life must first store up good things in his heart.

In the light of Matt 12:35, stated above, we can see that wealth and poverty are conditions of the heart first before it reflects in the life of a person. You can literally sense poverty from the way a person thinks whether he has money in his bank account or not.

Just as the medical doctor has been trained over the years until she now thinks, talks, and breathes medical science, so the truly rich person is one who has trained her mind to think, talk, and breathe wealth. She does not see herself as poor even if there is no food on the table.

When you have truly adjusted your thinking and you begin to see yourself as wealthy, you will begin to see opportunities to create the wealth. But the man who sees himself as poor in his thinking will reject opportunities even when they are staring at him in the face. You cannot attract wealth if wealth is not found on the inside of you.

I don't know who said it but it is very true, "The heart of the matter is a matter of the heart." The heart is the sum total of the internal make-up of the man which is primarily the thought pattern of the man.

HOW DOES MY THOUGHTS AFFECT MY LIFE?

Zig Ziglar said, "You cannot consistently perform in a manner that is inconsistent with the way you see yourself." Your world is a reflection of who you really are on the inside. You attract who you are, not just what you want. If you want it, first become it. When you are it, then it has no choice but to come to you. An understanding of this principle already gives you a head start in life.

A magnet attracts metallic objects. But when the metallic object is bigger and heavier than the magnet, it can no longer attract it. Therefore it becomes necessary that to attract a bigger or heavier object the capacity of the magnet must be increased because its capacity determines what it can attract.

In the same way, the capacity of your mind determines what you experience in your life. Humans are not cast on stone. When people say, "That is just the way I am," it is due to a lack of understanding of who they really are. That is not the way you are, it is how you have chosen to be. And the day you choose to change you will change. I repeat, the day you choose to change you will change.

BEING PRECEDES DOING

About 2,000 years ago, a member of the Jewish ruling council by name Nick, who had studied a seemingly ordinary man do great things was amazed and decided to pay this man a visit. Because of his status in the society he was ashamed that he would be seen by others, so he decided to go by night. When he met him, the following conversation ensued;

Nick: No man can do these things…
Man: Except a man be…

Of course, you know the story is that of Nicodemus and Jesus in John Chapter 3:1-3. But isn't it an eye opener when you look at it this way? No man can DO… except a man BE. BEing precedes DOing.

Nicodemus was focusing on what Jesus was DOING. But Jesus made him realize that it is not just about doing. It is about BEING. It is who you are that drives what you do. If what you are doing is not already a part of you it is only a matter of time before it becomes obvious.

The medical doctor is first TRAINED to BE a medical doctor before she begins to treat (DO) people. She does not begin to treat people before she becomes a doctor. The teacher is first trained to BE a teacher before she starts teaching. Same goes for the engineer, the lawyer, etc. The essence of the training is to make them BECOME.

Personal Transformation and Leadership - Part 2

Keys to Transformation.

1. Think Possible.

God never thinks impossibility.

Mark 10:27

"...for with God all things are possible." (KJV)

The quality of your life will be determined by the quality of your thoughts. And since the battle is in the mind you must constantly fight to ensure that your thoughts are in line with what God says.

When all your life you have always lived in deprivation and want, when you have to use knife to cut the toothpaste so you can maximize the paste in the tube because of lack of money in the family it becomes difficult for such a person to believe that he can live a life of abundance.

The process of beginning to think like God is one that has to be deliberate. So when depressing thoughts come to you, you make a deliberate switch to things that are lovely, right, honourable, etc. I am not saying it is going to be easy, especially when the facts are staring at you in the face, but you can do it. You can make that switch.

You make that switch when you constantly remind yourself about who you really are. You are in the image and likeness of

God. You are already like God therefore you should not think impossibilities. Even though it seems like the walls are closing in on you, you remain focused and continue to think possibilities. You must never have a defeated mindset because you are already in the likeness of God and God CANNOT be defeated.

2. Take Responsibility for The Way You Feel
God is not depressed or discouraged.

Ps 16:11
"In Your presence is fullness of joy;" (NKJV)

How you feel is usually born out of your thoughts. So your feelings let you know if your thoughts are right or not. If you are feeling depressed it is because you are thinking depressive thoughts. And we know that God cannot be depressed. My dominant personality trait is the Melancholic trait. So I know a lot about mood swings. But your personality does not have control over you. You have control over your personality.

Some people say they feel sad because things are not working. So they remain in a sad and depressive state for weeks. But the bible says in Prov. 15:15 "…happy people always enjoy life." (TEV). It does not say those who enjoy life are always happy. That is what the WORLD says, but God's word says it is those who are happy that will always enjoy life.

Therefore, if I want to enjoy life, I place myself in a happy state.

A great speaker would say, "It is not because things are bad that you are sad, it is because you are sad that things are bad." You can choose to be happy even when things are not working. Someone said if you change the way you are looking at something, what you are looking at will change.

If you are sad when you don't have money and happy when you have money then you really don't have control over yourself. What that means is that money is what is controlling you. It's very obvious isn't it? But move into your day like all is working for you and in no time you will be amazed at how things will turn.

Life is beautiful if we will only follow the template God has placed down for us. The way of this world is directly opposite to the ways of God. If we want to maximize our lives we must have a paradigm shift.

All these excuses of "so and so person is making me feel bad is directly opposite to the life God wants us to live. How you feel is your responsibility. I repeat, "HOW YOU FEEL IS YOUR RESPONSIBILITY." Placing the responsibility of how you feel in the domain of other people is giving others the control over your life. If I can control your feelings then you are my puppet.

Stop giving these kind of excuses, "it is because of what this or that person said or did that is making me feel bad." You don't have control over what a person will say and how he or she will say it. Always remember that. What you have control over is how you will respond to what has been said. Are you going to allow what the person said or did to affect the rest of your day, or you are going to let it bounce off your skin? I prefer the latter than allowing one useless comment ruin my entire day.

In other words, you can choose to go to work tomorrow and you will be a completely different person. That colleague that used to annoy you will no longer have that power because you have the power to decide how you want to react even if the colleague is doing annoying things. The power is with you. Take responsibility.

3. Say The Right Things

If you read the story of creation as related in Genesis chapter one you will find that the first words God spoke were the words "Let there be light," in the King James Version.

Gen 1:3
"And God said, Let there be light:" (KJV)

The original Hebrew text what God actually said was, "Light, be!" God was not negotiating or making a request. He was not complaining that the darkness was too much. He spoke what He wanted to see. He issued a command.

So in your journey to Personal Transformation and Leadership you must not let your external realities shut you up. Speak to your external realities with authority. Issue commands to the circumstances around you. Even when it seems like nothing is changing, do not stop, do not doubt. Keep at it. Remember you are making a switch from a former way of life to a completely new one. You must therefore be patient with yourself in this journey.

Speak positive things to yourself and about yourself, especially when you are alone or early in the morning. If you are prone to anger, say to yourself, "I am gentle, anger does not have control over me. I will be gentle with people even when they try to get me angry. I have control over my emotions."

Keep saying these positive words to yourself over and over till it registers deep in your subconscious. In a short while you will see changes in your own life. Things may not necessarily change overnight but as you continue, things will change.

4. See Things the Way They Should Be

God sees things the way they should be, not the way they seem to be. God sees possibilities. He sees potentials. How do you see yourself? Do you see yourself the way you seem to be or the way you should be? And keep in mind that the way you should be is the way God has already made you. If God had not seen light in Himself he would not have been able to issue the command for light to be. He first saw the light in Himself. Do you see light in yourself or is it all gloomy?

See good things about yourself. Envision a bright future for yourself. Don't look at your current situation. Keep painting a beautiful picture of yourself. Don't let lack of money alter your picture, See what you want.

5. Act Right

When you have learnt to think right by thinking possibility, take responsibility for how you feel, speak the right things, and constantly see yourself as the best, your actions will naturally fall in place. Nothing will be able to stop you. From the moment you wake up till the moment you go back to sleep you will be in control.

You will not be afraid of challenges. Mountains become stepping stones. This is where people begin to wonder what happened to you. The problem here is that many people think that the anointing oil will automatically get them to this step. They cannot be farther from the truth. No laying on of hands, no anointing oil, can bypass the principles put in place by God.

When the anointing of God rests on a man, it is what it finds on the inside of that man that it will work with. If the way the person thinks is still shallow, there is not much the anointing can do. When Saul was anointed to be King he became another man, but because who he was on the inside was far below the anointing placed on him, grace diminished.

But when David was anointed King, grace increased because who he was on the inside was already a million times bigger than who he was on the outside. Your external realities will always level up with your internal reality.

As you begin to apply these keys on yourself you will naturally begin to stand out from the crowd. Because in your personal time when no one is watching, these are the principles you practices (TRAINING). You are not doing it because you are trying to please men. You are just being who you already are. Remember, Personal Leadership is not about the man out there. It is about you becoming who God has already made you.

Work Session on Personal Transformation & Leadership

Question 1: What were the key things you learnt from the Personal Transformation and Leadership chapter?

Question 2: How are the things you learnt in the chapter important to you?

Question 3: In what way are they going to help you become a better person?

Question 4: What are the immediate changes you will effect in your behavior to reflect what you just learnt?

Question 5: Are there any questions you have regarding the chapter?

Please make sure to put down your answers to this work session.

Chapter Two

Personal Leadership and Goal Setting - Part 1.

We have looked at Personal Transformation & Leadership and how we should focus on areas where we have control over. In this course we will be looking at how we can apply Personal Leadership in achieving our goals.

Let me begin by saying a vision is not the same as a goal even though we sometimes use them interchangeably. A vision is your definition of how the world should be or better still how your world should be. A goal is an achievement towards the vision.

Somehow, because we are time based, we tend to set our goals at the beginning of seasons especially at the beginning of the year. We call them New Year Resolutions. They are basically goals we hope to achieve before the year comes to an end.

These goals can be categorized into several classes which include

Spiritual e.g. read through the bible
Physical e.g. lose weight
Mental e.g. read books
Career e.g. get a new certification
Health e.g. eat healthier foods

Community e.g. volunteer to care for the elderly
Family e.g. get new car for the family
Emotional e.g. practice self-control

... and several other categories.

The essence of these goals is to give us a greater sense of fulfilment in our lives. Unfortunately, by the statistics, out of every hundred people, 92 will fall back to status quo and never realize their goals.

Just like time management, goal setting has evolved over the years. Different generations have come up with different techniques toward achieving goals. But the question remains, how come despite all of the techniques and methods and planners that we have been taught about goal setting we still have such a high failure rate? The answer is what we will be discussing about in this chapter.

AUTOPILOT

Technology has evolved to the extent that planes can fly on auto pilot. Once the coordinates are imputed, the control system takes over and that plane becomes locked in on the destination the coordinates represent. It has no choice but to arrive there.

Our habits are the flight path to our destination which is our goal. So, the question is, is your flight path in line with the destination you hope to arrive at? Your habits answer that question.

So, like the chapter title indicates, we will be looking at how our habits impacts on our goals and how we can lead ourselves towards where we want to be.

Without leaving where you are seated right now I want you to answer the following questions.

Where are your shoes in your apartment?
Where is your bottle opener kept?
Where is your car key?
Where exactly is your kitchen knife?
Where is/are your comb(s)?

I could go on with ten more questions like the ones above but those ones are enough to make the point I intend to make.

For most people, which I believe includes you, you know the answer to those questions WITHOUT THINKING. Notice the phrase, "Without Thinking." Most people have a particular place where they keep those items. You may not even remember when you dropped it there but you ALWAYS find it there.

When I wake up in the morning, one of the things I do is to go to the kitchen and drink water. I don't have to be thirsty. I have successfully programmed myself such that when I wake up those coordinates kick in.

When you get to the point where you can do things without thinking we say they have become a habit or you are functioning on autopilot. When you've done something over and over again, after a while your brain stores that process in an "autopilot" section. A large chunk of our day to day lives is handled by autopilot.

There is a reason why we function on autopilot most of the time. It is because there is a limit to what willpower can handle at a time. Each time you engage in decision making, or utilize willpower you drain energy reserve. When you begin to drain more than can be supplied per time, you begin to feel stressed. That is why teams usually take breaks during brain-storming sessions.

An illustration I can use here is one of doing multiple task on your system that has a 1GB RAM. After a while you will observe that the system begins to hang because you are trying to force it to go beyond its capacity.

What the brain does is to filter the things you do again and again in the same way and move them to autopilot. So, instead of utilizing willpower anytime you need to do that task, your brain just presses REPEAT.

That is why you can be walking to the bus stop and answering a phone call at the same time and still arrive at your bus stop. You are actually on REPEAT mode while walking while your brain utilizes decision making in answering the call. This way you don't drain much energy.

Many of us fail in achieving our goals because we don't have the habits that will make us actualize the goals. What many of us set as our New Year resolutions are not really resolutions, they are goals. Most of these resolutions are usually in the format:

I want to be…..
I want to have….
I want to achieve….

The opening phrase already shows that they are not resolutions. You cannot resolve to be or have or achieve. You resolve to do.

For instance, someone says their New Year Resolution is to complete the bible. That is an achievement. That is not a resolution. Take a random study and you will find that most people with such goals never succeed in reading through. In fact, by the end of January, they have dropped out.

Let me remind you of something I said in the PTL lecture.

"The medical doctor is first TRAINED to BE a medical doctor…"
"The teacher is first TRAINED to BE a teacher…"
"The lawyer is first TRAINED to BE a lawyer…"

Did you take note of the phrase, "TRAINED to BE"? The essence of the TRAINING is to make them BECOME.

But training is an action word. Training connotes doing something over and over. But during the training no one is there. Training takes place in private.

So we can say the medical doctor was doing something to become a medical doctor.

Who we are is formed by what we do when no one is watching. (Just as you were not there when the doctor was being trained). By what we do over and over again when it seems like no one cares. We BECOME by DOING little things over and over again. That was why we established in the first lecture that you cannot suddenly manifest something that is not already on the inside of you.

How do we BE? By doing seemingly little things over and over again until it becomes our default state. Notice I used the phrase "seemingly little things." Because though they seem little, they are what really matter the most.

Aristotle said, "Men acquire a particular quality by constantly acting in a particular way. You become just by performing just actions, temperate, by performing temperate actions, and brave, by performing brave actions."

Public performance is the result of private practice.

Take a look at the following simple mathematical equations

$A + B = Z$

$A + B + C = Z$

$A + B + C + D = Z$

$A + B + C + D + E = Z$

$A + B + C + D + E + \text{---------------} + Y = Z$

There are infinite numbers of variables that add up to become Z. What many of us do is to say our goal is Z and we end there. We don't really come out with a resolution that will make the goal realizable. Even though we say we are making a New Year Resolution, they are actually not resolutions they are goals.

To resolve is to disintegrate, analyse, break up or separate into parts.

What does that tell us? Resolutions are what you do. So after coming up with our goals, the next step is to outline the resolution that will get us to our goals. That means the right thing would have been to say, "My resolution for 2017 is to DO A, or B, or C. Because when you do A, or B, or C, then you are on your way to achieving Z. But many of us just say our resolution is to achieve Z. It won't work that way.

A few years ago I was in debt to the tune of about three thousand dollars, $3,000. While my goal was to get out of debt I needed to come up with a resolution. My resolution was to pay (DO) $500 to my creditor(s) at the end of every month until I pay off the entire debt. And I did. I got out of debt.

Caroline L. Arnold said, "…You must define explicit actions to practice, one by one, until you begin to do them automatically."

I did not just wake up every morning, lay my hands on my head and declare, "I am out of debt, I am out of debt, in Jesus' name." Instead I defined explicit actions to execute that got me one step closer to getting out of debt. All through scriptures the power of God kicks in when men defined exactly what they wanted to do.

Now, let's take some more hypothetical examples of our usual resolutions:

I want to BE more loving
I want to BE more organized
I want to finish the bible
I want to GET OUT of debt
I will LOSE weight
I will QUIT smoking
I will BE neat

I believe by now it is easier for you to see what is wrong there. Those are goals, not resolutions. What does "more organized" actually mean? What will be the indicator that you have become more organized?

Let's take NEAT as an example. To be neat includes all of the following and more.

Keep the sheets clean and unruffled
No plates left in the sink overnight
Clothes not littered on the couch in the sitting room
Prescriptions kept in the medicine cabinet
Shoes on the shoe rack
Car key kept in designated position

….and many more.

For someone else, being neat could generate an entirely different set of list. In the same vein, "I want to be more loving" will generate its own list of what it means to be more loving. Therefore, just saying your resolution is to be more organized is actually an abstract term and you cannot chase the wind.

So also, does "finish reading the bible." What exactly do you mean? Do you mean you will read 10 chapters every Saturday or 2 chapters every day? If it is 10 chapters every Saturday, when on Saturday? Morning, afternoon, or evening? So just saying you will finish reading the bible is not good enough.

AUTOPILOT RESISTS CHANGE

It has been established that most of the time what we do is what we do most of the time. A large chunk of what we do, we are actually doing on autopilot. This is also why we fail when we resolve to be Z instead of resolving to do A. When we resolve to be Z we immediately want to do all the variables that make up Z but autopilot says "NO! That is not how I have always done it." Autopilot resists change.

Because there is only so much willpower you can muster per time, you soon begin to feel drained as you try to get so many things done at one time, all in a bid to lose weight, or be more organized or to get out of debt - whatever your goal may be. Any wonder why by the month of April more than 50 percent of people have abandoned their New Year resolutions.

What if there was a better way? What if we can actually take advantage of autopilot and use it for our benefit?

CONVENTIONAL GOAL SETTING APPROACH.

If you work in the average organization where there is more than lip service to training and development, you are likely to have done training on goal setting. The common formula or steps taught is the popular SMART method. In case you are not familiar with it I'll just do a quick summary.

S – Specific: The goal should be definite, not vague or ambiguous
M – Measurable: There must be a way to rate it. Percentage completion
A – Attainable: The goal should be within reach

R – Realistic: It should be something real

T – Timely: The goal should be tied to a specific time frame

The problem is that most of the time this method works well with corporate organizations. But when it comes to your personal goals they hardly work. Mostly because you are accountable to no one. You can see why even though many people use that approach in their personal goals they don't get the desired result.

Personal Leadership and Goal Setting - Part 2

This is the continuation of "Personal Leadership and Goal Setting - Part 1"

THE SEVEN EASY STEPS

I shared with you how I used a simple approach to pay down almost half a million debt. As at the time I never knew there was another method besides the SMART method. I just came up with that system because it was:

Easy: I did not struggle to do it. $500 a month was relatively easy for me.

Measurable: I was going to be paying $500 monthly. Not $200, not $700.

Instant reward: I felt a sense of burden lifted immediately I paid off the $500 each month.

Personal: I came up with what I can do by myself not what a book suggested.

Resonated: Paying $500 per month felt good to do. Not too little, not too much.

Trigger: Receiving the little income I was earning was a trigger to immediately pay off $500.

Light burden: I did not feel a heavy weight on me as if I was trying to do so many things at a time. I focused on one creditor per time and moved on after I had finished with that one.

Then a few years later I read a book by Caroline L. Arnolds, Small Move, Big Changes. She explained in the book the very same method I had used to pay off my debt a few years ago.

In summary, this was what she said in the book.

1. Resolutions should be easy to do
2. Resolutions should be explicit and measurable actions
3. The results should be immediately felt
4. Resolutions should be personal
5. Resolutions should resonate
6. Resolutions should be triggered
7. Resolutions must be few at a time. (Caroline L. Arnolds recommends maximum of two)

It does not matter whether you are finding it difficult to read a book to the end; build a better relationship; learn a new skill; be organized; trying to deal with the habit of complaining; get to work early; trying to lose weight (or maybe add weight); clearing your mail box; whatever habit is that you want to stop or cultivate, using these seven steps will get you there.

Remember that equation we saw earlier were Z is where or what you want to BE. But A, B, and C are what your resolution should be about. Never make the right side of the equation your resolution. People who focus on the right side of the equation hardly achieve their goal. People who focus on the left side of the equation hardly fail in achieving their goals.

When applying this seven step approach in goal setting, because the resolutions are easy to do you may want to make several resolutions at a time. But research has also shown that it is best to keep it low. Different experts proffer different numbers. Caroline L Arnolds actually advises not more than two at a time. I, personally have never done two at a time. I always focus on one per time until that one has become a habit then I can come up with another resolution.

The frequency of the action contained in the resolution determines how long it will take to become a habit. A resolution to drink 2 glasses of water per day, or to do 5 push-ups every morning will not take too long to become a habit, probably 2 or 3 weeks, because of the frequency of occurrence - everyday.

But a resolution where the frequency is lower, say once or twice a week may take a longer period to become a habit, probably 1 or 2 months. The whole exercise is not so you can cover so many resolutions at the end of the year, but that you actually develop new habits that will become part of your life.

Now, let's come up with an average time frame it will take to cultivate a new habit. Let's say 1 month. That means at the end of the year there would have been 12 changes in you. Believe it or not, that is profound. Statistics indicate that more than 50 percent of people give up on their resolutions by April.

And by July more than 80 percent have given up. What does that mean?

It means by April people who said they were going to achieve this or that actually fall back to status quo. They go back to the way they were doing things. Their autopilot did not allow them to change because they wanted to do so many things at a time. But if you only change one bit at a time you are exercising personal leadership on yourself and before you know it you have become a completely changed person.

Now, let's really dig in on how someone can really experience a complete change in habit.

Let's say John has issues with neatness. He grew up in a home where there was really not much emphasis on keeping things tidy. When he returns home from school he dumps his uniform on any available space, most likely on the chair in the sitting room. He never bothers about making his bed. A pile of clothes is in the wardrobe from where he sorts out which to wear. Both the ones he has already worn and the ones not yet worn are all together. Am I painting a picture of someone who is really, really, not into neatness? I hope I am.

John is now a full grown man and that habit has grown with him. He lives alone and the moment you step into his apartment you don't need a prophet to tell you what sort of a person lives here. He is beginning to receive feedback about the state of his apartment. John has decided to change the habit.

So he writes down his overall objective, "I want to be neat." Then he realizes that is the right side of the equation and he decides to make a list of the variables (the left side of the equation). See the list below:

Keep the sheets clean and unruffled
No plates left in the sink overnight
Clothes not littered on the couch in the sitting room
Clothes should be hung in the wardrobe
Clothes already worn should be at the left side of the wardrobe
Books should be on the bookshelf
Remote control beside the TV when not being used
Shoes on the shoe rack

Remember that none of these is currently a habit. His autopilot is presently programmed to do the exact opposite of all of these. He is OK with sleeping on ruffled sheets. He does the dishes only when there is no more space in the sink. When he returns home from work he dumps his shirt on the couch. The list goes on.

These are his present default state. There is no way he can move from his current state to the being neat overnight. And if he attempts everything on that list all at once he will never make it beyond a few days.

What does John do? He picks up one of the items on the list and comes up with a resolution.

"I will make the bed first thing in the morning, everyday" or "I will make the bed before I go to sleep because I sleep better when the bed is made." He can frame it in the best way to make it resonate. And based on the resolution he starts making the bed either in the morning after he wakes up or just before he goes to sleep, depending on the resolution.

The first few days it is going to seem like work because this is not his default state, but at the same time it is easy enough for him to want to keep at it. By the second week it has begun to feel natural, and by the third week, what seemed like work 3 weeks ago is now a habit.

However, he does not bother about the plates in the sink, or the clothes on the couch, or the shoes that are flung under the bed. The resolution has nothing to do with those. It was just about the bed. But how do you think John felt each time he came home in the evening and met a clean bed? He felt good, really good.

After 3 to 4 weeks he has successfully swapped one bad habit for a good habit. Making the bed is now on autopilot. He does not need to remind himself. Now he can move on to another habit. He decides to pick on clothes not littered on the couch.

The next day he returns home from work and habitually unbuttons his shirt and flings them on the couch. What happens next? He remembers his new resolution which is, "I will hang my shirt in the wardrobe immediately I take them off so the sitting room can look tidy."

So he reluctantly picks up the shirt and any other clothing that is in the sitting room and walks into the bedroom and hangs them in the wardrobe. When he walks back to the sitting room, a different picture greets him. The sitting room looks much better.

Yes, the remote control is on the floor beside the chair where he sat to watch television the night before but he is not worried. His resolution was not about remote control, it was about clothes on the couch. He has passed. The bed in the room was made when he woke up in the morning. And now there are no clothes on the couch in the sitting room. Believe it or not, John is becoming neat.

Now, if John picks up one item on the list every 4 or 5 weeks what do you think will happen in about 6 or 7 months' time? You will walk into John's apartment and you will not believe it is the same John.

There won't be any plates in the sink. The bed is made. No shirts dumped on the couch. Clothes are arranged in the wardrobe. He has even bought a basket for dirty laundry. There is now a place for everything and everything is in its place. And he changed without feeling stressed. That is exercising personal leadership.

Now let's see if the resolutions John made are in line with the seven steps.

Resolution: I will make the bed first thing in the morning after I wake up.

1. Resolutions should be easy to do. Making the bed is not that hard. Doing everything at the same time would have been hard.
2. Resolutions should be explicit and measurable actions. Make the bed first thing in the morning.
3. The results should be immediately felt. Once the bed is made it is obvious. If it is not, it is obvious.
4. Resolutions should be personal. John came up with the resolution himself
5. Resolutions should resonates. Each time he made the bed he felt good.
6. Resolutions should be triggered. First thing in the morning. Once he wakes up the next thing is to make the bed.
7. Resolutions are few at a time. John was doing one at a time.

Now you can see that as simple as the statement was it met the seven steps.

You, also can apply this approach in your personal life and whatever you aim to achieve will become possible if you follow these easy steps. It all boils down to Personal Leadership.

Work Session on Personal Leadership & Goal Setting

The following questions are meant to assess our level of understanding of the Personal Leadership & Goal Setting lecture. Kindly answer them by putting down your answers.

Question 1: What were the key things you learnt from the chapter?

Question 2: How are the things you learnt in the chapter important to you?

Question 3: In what way are they going to help you become a better person?

Question 4: What are the immediate changes you will effect in your behavior to reflect what you just learnt.

Chapter Three

Entrepreneurial Mindset - Part 1

Entrepreneurial Mindset, simply put, is about the mindset of Entrepreneurs. In this course we will be learning about developing the mindset of Entrepreneurs. But first, we need to know who an Entrepreneur really is.

According to Len Schlesinger, President, Babson College and Harvard Professor. "An Entrepreneur is someone who makes and finds opportunities to create economic and social value everywhere."

Entrepreneurs are 'ORDINARY' people who make and find opportunities to create economic and social value everywhere. The keyword here is "ORDINARY." Nobody is born an entrepreneur. People "become" entrepreneurs.

Peter Drucker said, "Most of what you hear about Entrepreneurs are all wrong. It's not magic, it's not mysterious, and it has nothing to do with genes. It's a discipline, and like any other discipline, it can be learned."

Entrepreneurs are not born, they are made.

What we will be focusing on in this class is to make an entrepreneur IN us. To be able to THINK, and hence, address issues from an entrepreneurial perspective.

This is necessary because whether you currently run a business of your own or are currently employed, having an entrepreneurial mindset is the key to growth. Someone who runs a business of her own but still thinks like the average employee will have a stunted growth, while an employee who thinks like an entrepreneur will experience a sharp rise in his or her career.

WHY THINK LIKE AN ENTREPRENEUR?

Thinking like an entrepreneur has a lot of merits, some of which are stated below:

1. Thinking like an entrepreneur creates a paradigm shift on why private companies are run differently from the way government establishments are run. Entrepreneurs always maximize resources, using minimum input for maximum output. They are not wasteful. While governments spend, private companies save. Entrepreneurs solve problems profitably. So they are very mindful of their spending. Resources must be properly accounted for and utilized judiciously.

2. Thinking like an entrepreneur frees one from an "employee mindset" even if one is an employee. There is nothing wrong in being an employee, but there is something wrong in retaining an employee mindset all your life. Just as there is nothing wrong in being materially poor, which is actually a

temporal state, but there is something wrong in having a poverty mindset.

The employee who thinks like an entrepreneur does not see management as the enemy. Those with employee mindset see every new policy from management as a plot to further worsen the state of the employees but when you begin to think like an entrepreneur you get to see things from a different perspective. You see from the other side of the fence. Some policies are necessary for the organization to remain profitable.

3. Thinking like an entrepreneur places you in control of yourself while still working for someone else. Mohammad Yunis, Nobel Peace Prize winner, 2006, said, "We are all entrepreneurs, only too few of us get to practice it." Most employees think they are working for somebody. But the truth is we are all working for ourselves, every single one of us. When you begin to think like an entrepreneur, that truth dawns on you and it affects your outlook on the organization. You want to learn more and understand more about the business when you realize that you are working for yourself.

4. Thinking like an entrepreneur makes you develop interest in the core of the business. Every business has its core functions and its support functions. Wherever the employee who thinks like an entrepreneur is located in the organization, she always has an interest in the core function of that department and

how it ties into the core function of the organization. That is what keeps the business running.

When there is a loss in production time due to a breakdown, some people are happy to just go to the canteen or just rest or while away the time. But that is the company losing money. Those with an entrepreneurial mindset think differently. When one begins to think like an entrepreneur they get to see why such behaviors are inappropriate. You get to understand why private employers of labor are not happy when at every little thing the government declares a public holiday.

5. Thinking like an entrepreneur while still in paid employment keeps you in good health. Defective health is not just a function of physiological imbalances in the body. It is also the result of emotional or/and psychological imbalances. Health is a state of physical, psychological, emotional, and mental well-being.

Therefore, one's psychological perception of the state of things at the office can affect one's health. Most times, stress is really not only the result of too much work, it is also about our "perception" of work. When you cannot tie what you are doing to an overall objective you begin to feel stressed. People want what they do to have meaning.

The man who, once it's getting to 5:00pm, begins to look at the clock because he wants to quickly rush and leave the office, but is compelled to remain for another hour or two so some pressing needs can be resolved will not perform optimally because he feels he is being punished. But the man who thinks like an entrepreneur knows that he needs to invest some more time today, or once in a while, to resolve the pressing need so he can free up time for some other tasks tomorrow. That simple shift in mindset can affect the kind of hormones the body releases.

Mind you, I am not saying one must keep spending three to five hours every day after work at the office. That could mean you are in the dangerously over-challenged zone. You are living in crazy-land. But occasionally, maybe during a project or some other pressing need, one may need to put in extra hours.

6. Thinking like an entrepreneur gets you a fast rise in your career. The employee who thinks like an entrepreneur will be making contributions during meetings that top management will be interested in because her suggestions increases the company one way or another. Remember our definition? "Makes and finds opportunities to create economic values..."

And when the company grows, the people also grow. She does not just bring suggestions that will benefit only the junior staff because she is one, but rather brings suggestions that will benefit the organization and increase the profit of the organization. When the organization makes profit the people benefit from it and everyone goes home happy.

The person who comes up with ideas that will save cost for the company has placed a spotlight on herself already. In subsequent meetings, management will want to listen to her. And in no time she becomes part of management herself.

7. THINKING like an entrepreneur prepares you for the ROLE of an entrepreneur. If one is not mentally prepared for anything, chances are that person will find it hard becoming successful in it. You cannot go where your mind has never been.

There are countless number of people who make the mistake of leaving their paid employment into self-employment without being mentally prepared for the role. They think being self-employed is an escape route from working hard. They think it's a status upgrade. What they don't know is that they just changed jobs and because they are now both the employer and the employee, they just compounded their predicament.

If one has not developed the mindset of an entrepreneur while still working for an organization, it will be very difficult to sail through if he or she leaves the organization to become self-employed. The one who has developed the mindset of an entrepreneur is better prepared for the challenges that face a self-employed person.

8. Thinking like an entrepreneur helps you know when to let go of non-productive activities. Not everything we do really adds value to the overall objective of the organization. And to

maximize resources you need to identify the non-productive areas. That is why companies can shut down departments and decide to outsource the jobs. That is why downsizing takes place during critical economic conditions so the company can stay afloat.

The average employee does not understand. These are hard decisions but necessary for the organization to stay alive. One of the roles of the business owner or entrepreneur is to hire and fire. And emotions must not get in the way of carrying out this function otherwise your ship will soon sink. You must learn to hire and fire. It is a must for anyone who must make significant impact. When a part of the body is gangrenous, doctors amputate that part so the rest of the body can stay alive. Otherwise, soon, the entire body dies. When you start thinking like an entrepreneur you will understand the reason for certain hard decisions that are taken by your organization and it will also help you in making hard decisions, too.

Entrepreneurial Mindset - Part 2.

This is the continuation of "Entrepreneurial Mindset - Part 1"

Here, we will be looking at the qualities or behaviors of entrepreneurs. Most books tend to hype these qualities as though they were superhuman qualities that only a select few ever get to possess. My objective here is to let us see that they are not really any superhuman qualities. Instead they are qualities that every human has. The only difference is the extent to which we practice them. What are some of these qualities?

1. Visionary
Entrepreneurs are visionary. Sam Adeyemi says, "A vision is a mental picture of a preferable future." It is the ability to see into the future what you want to be or have. Jesse Duplantis said, "If you cannot see a future, you cannot have a future." Now, what is the requirement for vision? The only requirement is imagination. As long as your imaginative ability is functional you can always come up with a vision. Then you can now set a goal and come up with a plan and milestones to reach. The beautiful thing is that even a blind man can imagine. So, one does not need the physical eyes to be a visionary. I am pretty confident that every human being has imaginative ability. We use that ability every day, therefore, it cannot be the exclusive reserve of a select few.

2. Innovative

What do you do when driving and you notice that there is beginning to be too much traffic on your current route? You find another route with less traffic. Almost everybody does that, it is instinctive. That is innovation. Finding something and figuring out a way to do it better. Innovation is not necessarily about creating something new from scratch. That is invention. Innovation is also improving on what is currently in existence. We do this every day. When we observe that we are spending too much time on a task or an issue we find a way to do it better or faster. So, naturally, we are innovative. It is not one special quality that a special group of people have.

3. Passionate

Entrepreneurs find something they love or want and they go after it with everything in them. It is also called "will." They have the will to go after what they want. Entrepreneurs know that passion is as good as currency. And I am pretty sure you can identify with that. People hardly turn down a man with passion.

You can definitely think of times in your life when you went after something you really wanted, even if it was going after that pretty lady, your wife, or saving for that designer shoes or bags. That was passion at work. It does not mean you will always get what you are passionate about, but you will never get what you don't have any passion for. However, what many of us forget about being passionate is that we don't necessarily have to like every single process we go through while trying to achieve the objective we are passionate for.

Say, a guy, who is naturally not the calling type, sees a lady he really likes and wants to woo her. Even though he naturally does not like calling people, he will have to do that because it becomes a necessary skill in acquiring his set objective. That is also what entrepreneurs do. In going for what they want, they discipline themselves to acquire the necessary skills that will get them closer to their set objective. Those who only do the things they like will always be below those who do what they NEED to do to get the result they want.

4. Flexible

Nokia is known today for GSM phones. Well, maybe I should say "was known" since it has been bought over. But Nokia started as a wood-pulp mill in southern Finland manufacturing paper. And over the years they produced foot wears, tyres, rubber-bands, industrial parts, raincoats, etc. until they became known for GSM phones. They were flexible enough to know when seasons changed and they changed also.

Procter & Gamble has over 300brands in the market (www.pg.com),
Diageo, owners of Guinness, has 14 different brands (www.diageo.com),
Heinz, makers of Ketchup, has over 90brands (www.heinz.com/our-food/products/north-america.aspx),

Now, what about you? Some of you are currently working in areas completely different from your field of study. And you are doing very well in it. You are flexible too. If you were very rigid, not willing to change, you may be out of a job by now. So, in a way, you are flexible too. It's a quality we all have.

5. Leadership

This is the ability to inspire an individual or a group of people to achieving worthwhile goals. The issue of leadership is one quality that can split a room in halves. Are leaders born or are leaders made? That debate has been on for ages. This is a school for personal leadership. The very fact that we are here means we believe we can LEARN TO LEAD ourselves from where we are to where we want to be. That alone proves leadership can be learned. And I am very sure there have been times when you had to lead a group of people to achieve a specific goal.

6. Gut

Entrepreneurs sometimes move when all evidences are saying the contrary because of that inner conviction in them. Gut is the courage and determination it takes to do something unpleasant. It is this quality that makes them come across as being egotistical because it appears as if they don't listen to advice. Contrary to what everyone else is saying, they move on.

This trait is not an everyday trait. It is something they do when they have that inner conviction. You also can identify with that feeling when you suddenly know within you that something will work out even when the evidence seem contrary. We all have had such moments.

7. Persistence

This is staying power, lasting existence, endurance or durability. Your ability to remain. The Oxford Advanced Learner's Dictionary defines Persistence as "The act of continuing to try to do something despite difficulties especially when other people are against you and think that you are being annoying or unreasonable." Persistence keeps companies from going extinct. But this is also a trait that we possess as individuals. Right from our childhood days we can recall the many times we persisted just to have our way with our parents. We've always had this quality in us. However, note that facing the same challenge over and over again is not persistence. That is lack of knowledge.

8. Street Sense

Every economy has its rules. Every business has its secrets. Street sense comes in during the application phase of principles. We could also use the word "Technique." This is why it is better to learn principles than to learn techniques. Applying the same technique someone else used in another clime may not necessarily work for you. But the principles always work.

Once you've known the principle you can decide what technique to apply. You cannot apply the same techniques used in the first world nations in the third world nations. While principles work anywhere, street sense, is limited to location. So a successful entrepreneur must have the street-sense of his present location tailored for his business.

Of course, these are not all the qualities of an entrepreneur, but like it was stated earlier, these are qualities that we already possess. They are in-born.

You don't have to own a business of your own before you start seeing yourself as an entrepreneur. In your present places of employment you can start utilizing these qualities and start seeing yourselves as entrepreneur right where you are. We can start practicing being an entrepreneur long before we physically become one.

I believe with this chapter we now have a more balanced understanding about having an entrepreneurial mindset.

Work Session on Entrepreneurial Mindset

The following questions are meant to assess our level of understanding of the Entrepreneurial Mindset chapter. Kindly put down your answers.

Question 1: What were the key things you learnt from this chapter?

Question 2: How are the things you learnt in this chapter important to you?

Question 3: In what way are they going to help you become a better person?

Question 4: What are the immediate changes you will effect in your behavior to reflect what you just learnt?

Chapter Four

Redefining Purpose - Part 1

There seems to be a mystery beclouding the subject of Purpose. Was I born for a specific reason? How do I discover my purpose? How do I know I am fulfilling Purpose? And lots more. These and many other questions plague a lot of us. Many of us place our lives on hold, or so we think, in a bid to discover that thing called "Purpose."

In one extreme there are those who believe God must tell you what color of shoes to put on before you leave your house in the morning. Then, on the other extreme are those who go through life with a carefree attitude, without any sense of direction, as though life was one big parade on the beach. Even in a beach party you still need to be careful lest the waves suck you into the sea. The balanced life is somewhere between.

THE BEGINNING

"So God created man in His own image; in the image of God He created him; male and female He created them. Then God blessed them, and God said to them, "Be fruitful and multiply; fill the earth and subdue it, have dominion..." -Gen 1:27-28 (NKJV)

Truth is, man was created for a purpose and it is in the stated verse of the bible above. Here was God looking at mankind, eyeball to eyeball. Man just came out of the production line, so to say:

- Hardware? Check
- CPU? Check
- Memory Disk? Check
- Program? No program

This product does not know what to do. It is yet to be programmed. So God steps in with the codes to program him. He could have said anything to him but what did He program into man?

1. Be fruitful
2. Multiply
3. Fill
4. Subdue
5. Dominate

Those were the purposes given to man. Everything man does must be within the confines of those words.

The ULTIMATE purpose of man is to be fruitful. To be productive. Once you have this deeply engraved in you, life takes on a whole new meaning. I know that right now a lot of red flags are coming up in the minds of some of us because of the kinds of messages we have heard about purpose.

But let me ask you a question, have you ever seen the manufacturer of a product who hid the purpose of the product?

You go to a production line, see a new product being manufactured and you ask the manufacturer what does the product do, what is its purpose? And the manufacturer says he does not know. Does that make any sense?

Like Jesus would say, if we as humans know how to do certain things right why do we think God will now make us be at sea over why he created us? Well, just in case there are any doubts still in the mind of anyone then let's confirm from the New Testament if there is a portion that corroborates being fruitful as the purpose of man.

I think the best backing we can have will be Jesus' very words. Like Kenneth Copeland will always say, "Red words win." So, the very verses stated below were written in red if you have the red letter edition where the words of Jesus are written in red.

"Herein is my Father glorified, that ye bear much FRUIT; so shall ye be my disciples." - John 15:8 (KJV)

Notice He says the Father is glorified when we bring forth fruits, the same words used in Gen 1:28

"Ye have not chosen me, but I have chosen you, and ORDAINED you, that ye should go and bring forth FRUIT…" - John 15:16 (KJV)

Now, to ORDAIN is to "set apart for a purpose." And that purpose is to bring forth fruit. The same words used again. So, you find in the two verses stated above that the very same commission God gave man at creation was what Jesus repeated again. Bring forth fruits. Be fruitful.

So, where is the misconception coming from? Why is there so much confusion around the subject of purpose? It is because we have taken the means to an end and made it an end in itself. What many of us are actually calling Purpose today are not really purpose, they are just the means by which we are to go about fulfilling the ultimate purpose of man.

So, one man says his purpose is to preach another says his is to sing, or teach. No, those are just the gifts God has placed in us to fulfill the ultimate purpose of being fruitful. Being productive.

"God has given each of us the ability to do certain things well…" - Rom 12:6 (TLB)

"However, Christ has given each of us special abilities…" - Eph 4:7 (TLB)

"Why is it that he gives us these special abilities to do certain things best? It is that God's people will be equipped to do better work for him, building up the Church, the body of Christ, to a position of strength and maturity." - Eph 4:12 (TLB)

"As each of you has received a gift (a particular spiritual talent, a gracious divine endowment), employ it for one another as [befits] good trustees of God's many-sided grace." -1 Peter 4:10 (AMP)

So we can infer from the verses above that fulfilling purpose is not about being a pastor or being a doctor or being a teacher. You can be all of those and not fulfill purpose. You can be all of them and also fulfill purpose.

What you need to discover, rather, is what set of gifts you have been endowed with, to enable you fulfill purpose. Your gifts points you towards the area you will best accomplish purpose. If you really look deep within yourself you will discover that there are certain things you just do well. When you are locked in on those areas it's like the world comes to a halt.

There can also be someone for whom Engineering is just natural for him. Someone who just loves construction. Someone who is always thinking of how to design something to make life better for others. That person is also fulfilling purpose in that area.

I know that there are some people who can't really tell you where their natural strength lies. They don't know what their gifts are. What do you do when you are in such a situation? Get busy. Just do something, anything will do. You discover your gift in the process of doing something. As you begin to get engaged in doing stuff you begin to find out you just love doing some things much more than others.

Other ways through which one can discover their area of gifting include past experiences, what you have a natural flair for, what makes you cry anytime you come across it and you just want to solve the problem, something you feel is missing in your environment and you have a strong desire to fix, etc. All these and more are ways through which one can actually discover his or her gifting. But if you don't start doing something you may never find it.

In your quest to fulfill purpose you must realize that every phase of your life ties up with one another. Even the pain you go through has a role to play in your fulfillment of God's purpose. You must know that whatever you are doing today, even if it is not your ultimate role, then it has a relevant part to play in your ultimate role. You must, therefore, not be lackadaisical in whatever you are doing right now. Scriptures say in Eccl 9:10, "Whatever your hand finds to do, do it with all your might…" (AMP)

David's ultimate role was to be Israel's King, but tending for sheep was the training field through which he was going to be prepared. The experiences he had while tending the sheep gave him the courage to fight Goliath which brought him into fame in his country. And even though he was seventeen when oil was poured on him, it took him another thirteen years to finally get into God's ultimate role for his life, through which he was to fulfill purpose. And he was faithful in every enterprise he found himself involved in.

You must also know that the gifts we have is not just about the fivefold ministry of Apostle, Prophet, Evangelist, Pastor, and Teacher. Whenever some people hear the word 'Purpose' their minds just migrate to the fivefold ministry. But you can be in your role as a nurse, a teacher, an engineer, a banker, or a businessman and still fulfill purpose. Your role can be in that office you are in presently. Because Purpose is nothing but affecting lives. Making impact.

Redefining Purpose - Part 2.

This is the continuation of "Redefining Purpose - Part 1"

I am going to share two stories with you to elaborate and to buttress the point that you can fulfill purpose in any field. I will use Michelle Rhee (United States), and Mama Maggie Gobran (Egypt).

MICHELLE RHEE.

Michelle Rhee was one of the people featured in the 2011 Global Leadership Summit organized by the Willow Creek Association in the United States. She was interviewed by one of the organizers of the summit.

Michelle was 37 years old and a single mother of two when she was approached by the Mayor of D.C in 2007 to be the Acting Chancellor of the District of Columbia Public Schools. When she was approached by the mayor, she told him that she would only accept the role if the mayor was ready to place his entire political career on the line as she was not going to dance to the music of politicians. Her focus was going to be what was best for the kids. The mayor said he was ready, as long as what she was going to do would be the right thing for the kids.

Michelle accepted the offer and caused a firestorm. At that time, some schools were just 'Drop-out factories,' a term used for failing schools. There was a school that in over a forty year period, 60,000 kids had been admitted, but more than 40,000 of them never graduated from high school. And anywhere you have failing schools, the direct result will be failing neighborhoods. Michelle had the weight of the world on her shoulders.

But rather than bail out like many of her predecessors did, she went on and in one year she closed down 23 public schools including the school her own kids attended. It was a tough battle but she gave it her best fight. She fired a lot of school principals and reduced bureaucracy by 50%.

As at that time she was hated even by parents, so much so that the mayor was never re-elected. But after the dust had settled they realized that what she did was for the good of their children's future. She is now being celebrated. The movie 'Waiting for Superman' is about her reforms in the DC educational system.

MAMA MAGGIE GOBRAN.
Mama Maggie, like she is popularly called, was teaching at the American University in Cairo, Egypt, when she felt God's leading to care for the poorest of the poor in Egypt. That was what an aunt of hers did before she died.

The following Christmas she took gifts to the dump sites in Cairo where she found kids and very poor families living in the piles of rubbish. Her heart got broken. She resigned her job as a lecturer and set up an NGO named Stephen's Children, named after the Stephen of the Bible that was stoned to death.

From her background as an educator, she takes education to these children in the dump sites along with food, medicines and emergency relief materials, while bringing the gospel to them. Mama Maggie now has over 1400 staff members serving over 27,000 families in the dump sites weekly. Her background in the education sector is also helping her.

I used Michelle Rhee and Mama Maggie as illustrations so you get to know that fulfilling purpose is not about glamour. There are some tough callings.

Everybody cannot be a Pastor, speaking from the platform, but everyone can fulfil purpose if we just redefine purpose. Purpose is fulfilling the God-given mandate stated in Gen 1:28.

God never intended for Purpose to be shrouded in mystery. We were the ones that made Purpose appear mysterious. He made it very clear in Gen 1:28 what the purpose of man is. Be fruitful. Are you fruitful in your mind? Where is your brainchild? What about being fruitful in the works of your hands? In your tongue, do you speak positively? Are your words seasoned with grace?

What about being fruitful in your body? Are you multiplying? Are you replenishing? Are you subduing? Are you dominating the earth? Or do you just allow your emotions dictate everything you do? If whatever you are doing meets the above requirements then you are fulfilling purpose. The heavens are on your side. Whether you are in a paid employment or running a business of your own does not matter. What matters is that you are fulfilling your God-given mandate.

You don't need any external affirmation. And just in case you are feeling frustrated in your job, you feel like there is a wall between where you are now and where you should be then answer these questions John Maxwell always ask:

- What makes you cry?
- What makes you laugh?
- What makes you sing?
- What do you dream of?

If you can search deep within you and find answers to these questions then lunge forward with everything within you. Don't be afraid to take risks. It's better to try and fail than to live a life of regrets. And you never know until you try. Instead of asking "what if it does not work?" Ask "what if it works?" Whatever the mind can conceive the hand can achieve. If you can see it in you then you will hold it in your hands.

That was why we started with the Personal Transformation course. It does not matter whether you are 25 or 52, greatness is achieved not only by where you start and when you start but also by whether you start at all. Like Les Brown always say, "You don't have to be great to start; you have to start to become great."

This book is not really about how to discover your gifts. There are lots of books in the market that deals with such. This book is about us being grounded on what Purpose really is. There are so many misconceptions in this area that a lot of people who are actually fulfilling purpose feel like they are not fulfilling purpose because there is no glamour attached to what they do. But like we've seen, it is not about the accolades but about the results.

As we come to the end of this book permit me to say a short word of prayer for you.

I pray for you today that as you engage yourself in the fulfilment of your God-given mandate that you will not miss the mark. I pray that events in your life will nudge you to the place where you fit perfectly. To one it may be writing, to another it may be in engineering, to yet another it may be in politics, but in whatever area you will be at your best, you will find it. The heavens will see to it that you are always on track.

You will effect changes, not only in your immediate environment, but in the world at large. They may have said nothing good can come out of you, I say greatness will project from you. You will become a standard by which others will be measured. As you engage yourself in the area of your gift, the universe will align itself to favor you. And even though men may stand against you, they cannot stop you. You are already a success in Jesus' name. Amen!

Please go to Post 17 for the Work Session on this lecture.

Work Session On Redefining Purpose

Question 1: What were the key things you learnt from the chapter?

Question 2: How are the things you learnt in the chapter important to you?

Question 3: In what way are they going to help you become a better person?

Question 4: What are the immediate changes you will effect in your behavior to reflect what you just learnt?

www.ingramcontent.com/pod-product-compliance
Lightning Source LLC
Chambersburg PA
CBHW050016230526
45470CB00003B/995